The Top Ten

Lessons For Successful Business Leaders and Managers

Mandy Clark and Keith E. Smith

ISBN-13:978-1548351014

Winning Mindset Consulting

Visit Our Web Site
At
WinningMindsetConsulting.com

Table of Contents

"We all have dreams. But in order to make dreams come into reality, it takes an awful lot of determination, dedication, self-discipline, and effort."

~ Jesse Owens

Dedication

To all of the business owners and managers who make it happen, each and every day. We want you to know that your hard work and dedication do not go unnoticed. This book is for you.

We would also like to take this opportunity to thank our loved ones, Jenny and Justin, for their unwavering support and encouragement. There were many long days, and weeks, spent in the formation of these lessons. Their ongoing support made this possible. Thank you both.

Forward

If you a leader of a business, you likely picked up this book looking for ideas on how to improve your business. The lessons in this book will, if applied, lead you to your goals.

I have been in the customer service industry all of my adult life. I have been involved with hospitality management, technical support, billing support, and even waited tables. I took a six year break from working to raise my daughter, but afterwards I re-entered the workforce as a barista for a local coffee shop. Being a barista was not my ideal job, but at the time I just wanted to get out of the house and make some money. Later, I came to realize that I wanted more.

I first met Mandy and Keith in November of 2014 when they were co-managing a massage studio. I had quit my job as a barista and was looking for something that offered more opportunities for growth. I found out that a massage studio in my area was looking for front desk sales staff. I was interested, but a little hesitant since I knew next to nothing about the health and wellness industry, not to mention sales. I knew I had phone skills, but I had never received any sales training whatsoever. In fact, I detested sales and salespeople in general. I realized sales was a necessary part of any business, but I had no interest in ever becoming one of "them". I took a chance, interviewed for the job, and was hired! I was excited, but nothing could have prepared me for the transformation I was about to undergo.

Mandy and Keith could see my potential, and they allowed me to flourish. They supported and encouraged me the entire way using the very information you now hold in your hands. I have first-hand knowledge of how effective the lessons in this book are when it comes to transforming a business, and the people who work within it. I lived it and I know they work.

All of the lessons in this book are important, but there are three that stand out for me personally:

Lesson 1- Mindset: Keith was the first person to shift my mindset and focus. He helped me see that I wasn't just trying to sell something (in this case it was a monthly wellness program), I was simply educating the client about the best way to improve their overall well-being. Remember, I did not have the best opinion about sales, and they had to practically drag me kicking and screaming into it. And do you know what? I am so grateful they did. I am grateful to them for teaching me not to fear a sales position, to embrace it, and succeed at it!

Lesson 2-The Hiring Process: I experienced this myself, and saw others experience it too. If it happened that someone was hired who I felt was not a good fit for our team, I was able to go to

Keith, or Mandy, and express my opinion. They would listen to me, and my coworkers, and act in the best interest of our team. The morale and success of our team was always their highest priority.

Lesson 6- Micromanaging: As an employee, you do not want to be ruled with an iron fist, or be afraid to make a mistake. There were times we felt like that, but Mandy and Keith shifted that culture. Once the fear of making mistakes was gone, we began to grow. We definitely made some mistakes, but we also learned how to fix them and prevent them from occurring again. Mandy and Keith gave me room to grow, and they knew that they could count on me to do the right thing for the client as well as the business.

With Keith's positive attitude, and Mandy's support and fun personality, we worked together to turn that business around. It took hard work, training, and determination, but we succeeded where others had not. I was happy to be a part of that success, and I couldn't have done it without them. I would not be the effective and valuable employee that I am today without them and the lessons I learned. Now, you have those lessons in this book. I know they are important for any business owner, or manager, with a desire to transform their business.

Like I said before, I experienced all of the lessons in this book. I was there for the successes, and the hard times. Through it all I knew I could count on Keith and Mandy, not just as my managers, but as dear friends to guide me toward success.

Millie Case-Herndon
Sales and Customer Service Specialist

Introduction

We have been where you are right now. You want to make big things happen in your business, but you are not sure where to start, or how to get where you want to go. It took a lot of time and effort for us to develop solutions that work, and it took us years to achieve a breakthrough, but that does not have to be the case for you. This book contains the top ten lessons we learned as managers of a business, and they are the launching pad from which you can take your own business to higher levels of success.

A business is made up of people, and in order for a business to succeed people must work together as a team. This is where many companies encounter their greatest challenge because it is not easy to take a group of individuals and mold them into an effective team. The lessons in this book will not only help you build a team that will grow your business, they will also help to lower your stress and even have some fun along the way. These ten lessons were forged in the fires of struggle, on the front lines of business management, and they work. We have witnessed individuals become teams, closing ratios double, and the atmosphere within businesses transform.

You are passionate about your business and we are passionate about your success. We wrote this book so you would know that you are not alone and that you have options. At the end of each lesson you will find questions to ask yourself. They will help you evaluate your current team and environment, as well as create an action plan for reaching your goals.

ABOUT THE AUTHORS

Mandy and Keith come from completely different backgrounds. When they began working together in the same wellness business, they soon discovered they shared many things in common; a solid work ethic, drive, commitment to excellence, and a desire for personal growth. All of these qualities served to create an effective management style that resulted in an unprecedented level of success. The ten lessons in this book are the foundation of that success. Their success drew the attention of other wellness business owners and managers across the United States, all asking for help in growing their businesses. Today, Mandy and Keith put their unique blend of experience and expertise to work by helping these businesses grow to their true potential.

Mandy Clark grew up in the Chicago area, where she worked her way through college (sometimes working as many as four jobs) until finally earning a bachelor's degree in criminal justice. Though she had several family members serving as police officers, Mandy decided to move into emergency dispatching for fire and police departments. Her experience as an emergency dispatcher taught her the importance of established procedures, documentation, teamwork, and prioritizing tasks. Driven by her passion for helping people, she decided to move into massage therapy, going to school by day, and emergency dispatching at night.

For the first nine years as a massage therapist, Mandy worked as an independent contractor. She balanced operating her own business, while also working in a few chiropractic offices. In 2013 Mandy, along with her husband Justin, moved to Louisville, Kentucky. Soon after the move, Mandy got a job at a local massage franchise. She was hired as a massage therapist and within three months was the Lead Therapist. Before the year was out she was promoted to the therapist manager. Within two years of being hired she was the Operations Manager for the studio. The experience of working multiple positions inside a wellness business provided her a unique perspective that served her well in her role as manager of operations.

Keith Smith grew up in Frankfort, Kentucky. Being raised in a working-class family, Keith learned the value of hard work early in life. By the time he was fourteen years old, he was working his first job at a local country store, before eventually following in his father's footsteps and becoming an automotive technician. Two decades as a certified technician taught Keith how to quickly assess a problem, and then follow a diagnostic process that would lead to the cause as well as an effective repair.

These skills came in handy when he later moved into management. He also ran his own mobile, automotive repair business before pursuing different passions. Keith expanded his knowledge and skill in sales by attending the world-class sales training school of Combined Insurance Company in Chicago, Illinois. He relocated to Louisville, Kentucky where he found a job at a local massage franchise. Nine months after being hired he was promoted into management where his responsibilities included the hiring, coaching, and training of front desk sales staff. Keith is also the author of three books, and works as a part-time ghost writer for a Texas-based leadership and book writing company.

"Learning is not attained by chance, it must be sought for with ardor and attended to with diligence."

~ Abigail Adams

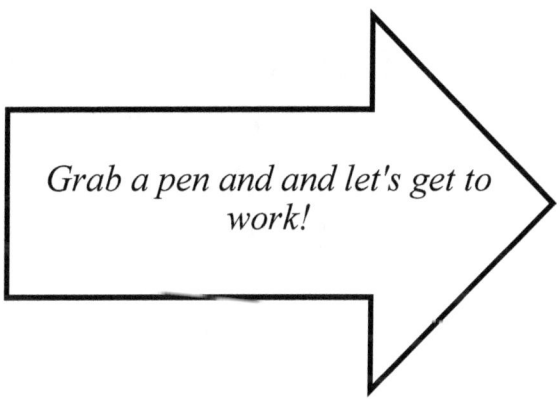

Grab a pen and and let's get to work!

"It all begins and ends in your mind. What you give power to has power over you."

~ *Leon Brown*
Former Outfielder for the Baltimore Orioles

Lesson 1

Mindset

Of all the lessons in this book, this is the most important one. Without a proper mindset, no amount of training or coaching will make someone a success. The challenge with this particular lesson is that no one can instill a winning mindset into another person. We all, as individuals, must make this choice on our own. However, once we have made the choice to shift our mindset, we can then seek outside guidance and help. This is why, as a business owner or manager, it is important to have a hiring process (more on this in lesson two) that helps you identify individuals who have a mindset conducive to learning, growth, and an overall positive view of life.

In order for your business to become successful, every person on the team must possess a winning mindset. That means the owners, managers, and employees must all share a similar attitude, and a desire to win. It is especially important for the management team to possess these qualities. At some point, there will be new people joining your team, and they will need to be trained by a person already equipped with the correct mindset. This is how you build a team of high performers.

There are two types of mindsets: Limiting and liberating. An individual who possesses a limiting mindset will see goals as difficult, or impossible, to reach. The person who possesses a liberating mindset will view a goal as a challenge and will search for ways to make it happen. You see the difference? One person sees the problem, the other sees the *possibility*. You can see why this the most important lesson. Everything else builds upon the mindset of the individuals involved.

Once, when we were both co-managing a particular business, we were tasked with growing the membership to a certain level. We both knew it was possible, and we both knew we were going to make it happen. We chased that goal for two years, and we tried everything. We had the best scripts, role played continuously, had meetings, tracked performance, and even tried huge bonus programs. Nothing worked, and we nearly lost our minds. Finally, we began researching the psychology behind winning sales teams, and realized what had been holding us back. Our team did not have a winning mindset, and overall morale was low. We set out to change that, and we did. Soon, we began breaking down barriers and reaching goal after goal. We built the membership of that business to a level higher than ever before, and the business had been operating for nine years.

Shifting the Mindset

You may find yourself in this situation: You have hired a team of people who have great attitudes and really want to do the best job possible. They are teachable and want to succeed, but they still have difficulty reaching their goals. So, what do you do when you have good people, but are stuck anyway? You shift their mindset.

If you are certain that you have hired the right team, but they still are not reaching sales goals, then it is likely your team members have differing views, low morale, or both. It could be that they have different ideas of what the goals are, how to achieve them, or what their role is in helping the team succeed. When the team is aware that they are not meeting expectations their morale will suffer (remember, how everyone feels, as individuals and as a team, will win out over everything else). To correct this you will have to shift the mindset of the team, as well as each individual. This may sound like a challenging task, but it is simpler than you may realize. In order to shift their mindset, you will have to shift their *focus*.

The pyramid on the following page illustrates how this works:

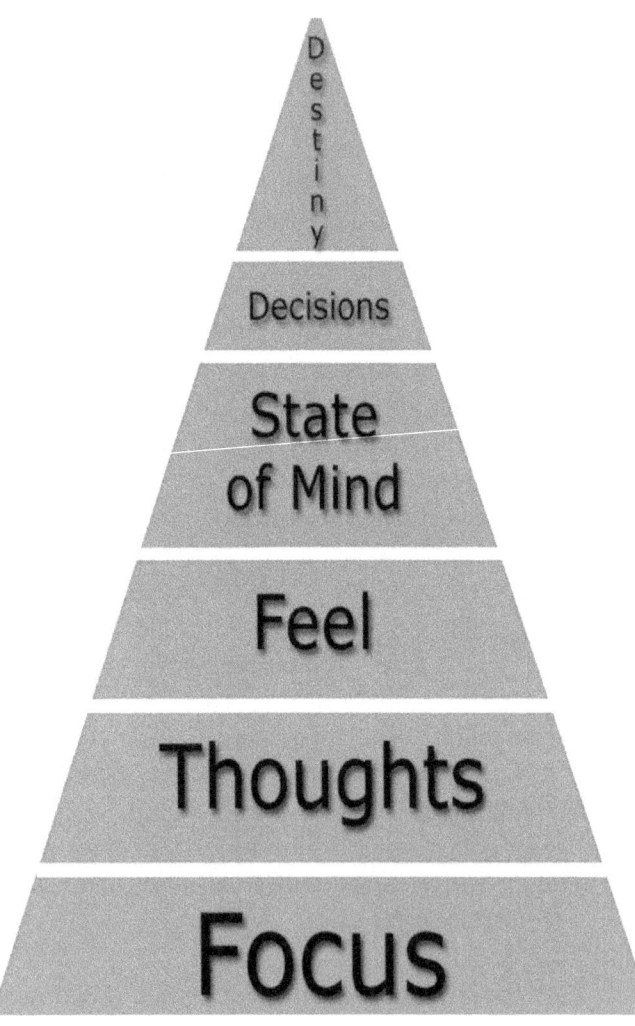

PYRAMID BREAKDOWN:

Focus: What you focus on, give your attention to, is the foundation for everything that follows. What you focus on the most will form your:

Thoughts: The thoughts that dominate your mind (the way in which you think) because of what you are focusing on most of the time, will determine how you:

Feel: Feeling trumps everything. It does not matter how well-trained you are if you feel miserable, stressed etc. The way you feel will determine your:

State of Mind: This is your mood. Your mood, good, bad, negative or positive, will strongly influence your:

Decisions: The power of choice, the decisions you make every day, will lead you in a certain direction. The direction depends on the quality of your decisions. Quality decisions will lead you to your:

Destiny: This is your end game. What you desire, your goals etc.

FOCUS

In order to shift the mindset of your team, you will have to get them all to focus on the same things.

Focus is the foundation upon which the pathway to goals is built. This is true both personally and professionally. In a professional context, your team's focus should be on job-specific skills and tasks. They will have to be completely clear on what their goals are, and the plan they will use to reach them. As the owner or manager, this responsibility falls on you. We recommend both group meetings and individual meetings in order for you to thoroughly solidify the primary focus of the team. Once you have successfully done this, the rest will begin to fall into place. When the team shares the same focus, they will share similar thoughts, feelings, moods, and will make effective decisions that will lead them to their goal. They will operate as one, and when that happens, goals will be reached. This process requires time and effort, but the results are worth it.

Hard work, effort, and persistence are all important components of success, but not as important as the underlying belief (winning mindset) that one is capable and in control of their destiny.

Real World Examples

Wrong Mindset: We once had a member of our staff that had three times the experience as everyone else on the team, management included. This individual also possessed more knowledge about the position, and knew the business well. However, this person had a defeatist mindset, saw the downside to every situation, feared accountability, and was terrified of responsibility. This person should have been one of the top performers on the team, but instead they were almost always at the bottom. They had received the same level of training and even more coaching, but to no avail. Others dreaded working with this person because it was a major drain psychologically. If this person had chosen to shift to a winning mindset, they would have been an amazing performer, and probably a great manager, but instead they ended up being fired.

Winning Mindset: We once hired an individual who was fantastic at customer service, but had no previous sales experience and was terrified of talking on the phone. As managers, we had been tasked with creating a sales culture. Like many people, this person did not have a positive view of sales, and was terrified of a performance-based pay plan. When the training began to heat up, this person did not react well and it looked as though they may quit. We spent a lot of time coaching and talking with them. After a few weeks, something within this person "clicked", and they began to shift their mindset. Soon, they began to be proactive, sought out help from peers, and made their desire to succeed known to us all. Fast forward a couple of months and this person had become THE top performer as well as the most skilled on the phone. It was an amazing transformation.

Lesson 1 Questions

- *Do you, and everyone on your team, have a mindset that is open to coaching and training?*

  Once you have evaluated how coachable everyone is, you may discover some who are unwilling to learn. If so, you will have to determine how that is affecting your team.

- *Does your team know what is expected of them?*

You will have a hard time shifting someone's mindset if they do not know what is expected of them.

- *Do you hold team and individual meetings?*

  Team meetings help build solidarity and cohesion. One-on-one meetings are beneficial too, especially if a team member wants to share something personal, or anything they do not feel comfortable sharing with the entire team.

Notes

Notes

"The smartest business decision you can make is to hire qualified people. Bringing the right people on board saves you thousands, and your business will run smoothly and efficiently."

~ Brian Tracy
Motivational Speaker and Author

Lesson 2

Hiring Process

Creating a hiring process that will help you select the best person for the job, and weed out those who would be a poor fit, will save you time, money, and a lot of frustration. More often than not, when you find yourself in need of a new team member, you need them fast. It can be tempting to rush through everything so you can fill the position as quickly as possible. However, taking this approach will usually result in a poor hire. You will then waste a lot of time and money trying to make the poor hire a good fit, only to end up firing them and starting the process all over again. There is a better way. When the time comes to fire someone it should be done swiftly, but that is not the case when hiring. Hiring, no matter how desperate you are, should be a slower process. In the end, it will save you a lot of time, and money.

The Job Ad

Start by creating a job ad that attracts the right applicants. A good job ad will help you in a couple of ways. First, it will help attract the right applicants. Second, it will help filter out those who may not be the best fit. Be sure to clearly define the position, and describe in detail the skills you are looking for in a candidate.

Once you begin receiving resumes, pay close attention to any details that can help you identify good and bad candidates. This process acts as a second filter to help weed out those candidates who would be a poor fit. A good resume' is typically one page, well written, and not filled with "fluff" disguised as applicable experience.

When you have identified a candidate you are interested in, we recommend emailing that person with further information about the position, the working environment and the culture of your business. Include in the email three dates and times that you would like to do a phone interview with them. The email acts as your third filter, and will further help you identify a good candidate. If a candidate does not respond, or cannot follow the simple instructions regarding the dates and times, you want to reconsider moving forward with them.

Phone Interview

When you and the candidate have agreed upon a date and time to do the phone interview, be sure that you have prepared yourself beforehand. Have some questions ready. For example:

- "What about this position interests you?"

- "What do you know about (the name of your business)?"

- "Do you have any questions about the information that I emailed to you?"

Face to Face

If you like the way the phone interview goes, set up a time to meet them face to face. If possible, when you do the in-person interview, have one of your teammates sit in with you. Your teammate can help to assess the candidate's body language and overall demeanor while you facilitate the interview. Be sure to choose a teammate that will give you an honest assessment of the candidate and whether or not they feel the candidate will be a good fit into your current culture.

Set a casual, but not too casual, tone to the interview so that the candidate will be at ease. Ask questions specific to the position for which you are hiring. Also, ask questions relating to their current, or past, jobs.

Here are some examples that will help you obtain valuable information about the potential hire:

- "Tell me about your current manager. What about their management style do you like and not like?"

- "What kind of incentive programs were in place at your last (or current) job? Was there anything about it you did not like?"

- "If I asked your manager about an area where you could benefit from some personal development, what do you think they would say?"

- "What expectations did you have going into your last job that were not met?"

These questions will reveal a wealth of information that will help you see how the candidate responds in various situations, and how they typically relate to management. Remember, you are looking for a certain skill set, but you are also looking for a particular *mindset* that will fit the culture of your business.

Keep in mind that the candidate is interviewing you as much as you are interviewing them. Here is where *your* mindset will be on display. If you project confidence, professionalism, positivity, and are friendly then the impression you make will be a good one. The same goes when you are offering the job to someone. Be excited, authentically, and positive.

Show them why working on your team will be a great experience, and they will accept your offer.

Real World Examples

No Solid Hiring Process: Experience is what taught us the value of a solid hiring process. We hired a lot of people, and many of them did not work out. When we were co-managing a massage studio, we were in desperate need of massage therapists. We hired one particular individual because he was very skilled, but we later discovered that his people skills were sorely lacking. This caused many issues with both clients and coworkers. It was not long before he was not showing up for shifts, and we had to fire him. We could have saved ourselves a lot of frustration if we had a solid hiring process at that time.

With Solid Hiring Process: After a few bad experiences with new hires, we created a hiring process that would land us the best people possible. It was not long before we reaped the rewards. We had lost a couple of people at the front desk of the studio we were managing. We needed people badly, but we had learned our lesson when it came to hiring too fast. We interviewed a few people, weeded out those we knew would not be a good fit, and eventually found the right person. She was part-time, but was soon selling the equivalent of a full-time person, and fit in nicely with the rest of the team. There is no telling how many people we might have gone through had we not taken the time to create a solid hiring process.

Lesson 2 Questions

- *Do you have an effective hiring process?*

  If not, we recommend taking the time to carefully put one together. It will help you find and hire the right people.

- *Is your job ad attractive to a potential hire?*

  Is it so wordy that it is being passed over? When someone is searching for a job, you want to be sure your ad stands out from the rest.

- *Do you have a list of questions prepared for phone interviews, and face to face interviews?*

  Preparing ahead of time allows you to focus on the applicant during the interview, rather than trying to think of what to ask them next.

Notes

Notes

"Definiteness of purpose is the starting point of all achievement."

~ W. Clement Stone
Businessman,
Philanthropist
And Author

Lesson 3

Clarify Goals

If you set out on a road trip without a destination in mind, will you get there? "Get where?", you ask. Exactly. If you set out on a journey, but have not chosen a specific destination, then it does not matter which direction you go. Wandering can be fun, unless it is happening in your business, and then it becomes expensive.

Clarity is determining exactly the results you want to achieve, and *when* you want to achieve them. Once you have determined your exact goals, and the timetable for achieving them, you must communicate that to your team. The only way to ensure that your team will reach their goals is if you make those goals crystal clear.

We witnessed the power of clearly defined goals firsthand when we were co-managing a membership-based wellness business. The front desk team was tasked with selling memberships, but there was not a clearly defined goal to meet. Each person was supposed to sell five, six, or seven, but no team goal had been set. There were goals that needed to be met in order for the business to succeed, but the individuals selling the memberships were unaware of those goals. Once we had clearly established monthly goals for each individual, and the entire team, memberships sales begin to rapidly increase. We began to track opportunities and conversion ratios, identified areas where more training was needed, and soon we were breaking records in that business. All of that was possible because we clarified the exact goals of the business, and then communicated those goals to each team member.

So, how can you develop clarity for your business goals? By asking yourself the right questions. Here are some examples of questions to ask yourself that will help you determine where you are now, and where you want to go. Only after you have that clarified can you develop an action plan to take you there.

"How do I define success for my business?"

"Where am I now?"

"Why am I here?"

"Where do I want to go?"

"What do I want to accomplish in the next ninety days? One year?"

"What do I need to focus on in order to reach my goals?"

"What do I need to change in order to achieve my goals?"

By knowing precisely what you want to achieve, you will know where to concentrate your efforts. Your goal must be clear and specific, and everyone on your team must understand the goal so that they can work together to achieve it. Clarity will help you more easily identify distractions, and will keep you moving in the right direction. Take the time to explain your vision to your team, and let them know what you want and why you want it. Doing this will help them understand the purpose behind the goals, and that you did not just snatch those goals out of thin air. As humans, we need to know the reason behind our actions, and if there is no clear reason there will be no clear action.

It is also important for your goals to be realistic, and that you give your team the necessary resources to achieve their objectives. Communicate to your team the timeframe within which the goals should be reached, and help them understand the benefits for reaching them. When your team has a clear understanding of the goals, the reason and benefits for achieving them, they will amaze you with their progress.

While we are on the subject of clarity, it is crucial that you create for your team a performance-based pay plan that is simple, and easy for them to understand. The more complex you make the pay plan, the less buy-in you will get from your team, and you may even lose some good people. Create a simple plan, and then stick to it. There is little that can cause more unrest in your team than a pay plan that never ceases to fluctuate.

Real World Examples

Without Clarification: As managers of a membership-based business, we had been tasked with increasing the number of members. In the beginning of our careers there, not one person on the team knew what the goals were. The owner had monthly, quarterly and yearly goals, but they had not been communicated to the team. It was no surprise to us that the goals were not being met. Each team member was supposed to have a minimum closing ratio of 20%. That is a pretty easy number to hit, yet their ratio was averaging around 11%.

With Clarification: The first thing we did was to meet with each team member, individually and as a group, and communicate to them exactly what their goals were. We did this both verbally and in writing, so there was no question about the expectations. In a matter of weeks we began to see significant progress. Sales went up and closing ratios rose to an average of 30%, and were often even higher. That is the power of clarification.

Lesson 3 Questions

- *Have you written down goals for yourself and the business?*

  Writing down your exact goals will help you achieve them. It brings clarity, and clarity is the first step to achieving goals. After all, if you do not know what you want, how can you get it? Once you have clear goals, you can then communicate them to your team.

- *If you have clearly define goals, does your team know what they are?*

  Your team can reach their goals, but only if they know what those goals are. Be sure to be specific.

- *Do the people on your team have a list of their own goals?*

Find out if the people on your team have personal goals, and then encourage them to achieve it. You will be amazed how this will positively affect your team.

- *Are your goals in alignment with the business? Are the personal goals of your team in alignment with the business?*

  It is okay for you, and everyone on your team, to have a list of personal goals. However, it is important to determine if those goals align with the business in which you are all working. If one feels as though their role within the business is hindering them from reaching their personal goals, then issues will arise.

Notes

Notes

---

*"Get to know
your employees,
and let them get
to know you."*

*~Lee Cockerell
Former Executive VP of
Walt Disney World Resort*

Lesson 4

Get To Know Your Team

One of the most important aspects of being in leadership is knowing your team members. It is common for many business owners, or their managers, to know little about a team member beyond their name and job description. However, taking the time to get to know your people on a more personal level will make a huge difference in morale, as well as your team's job performance. In lesson one we mentioned that how your team *feels* will win out over everything else, and it is true. You can have the best training program available on the planet, but if your team is not happy, no amount of training will help your business succeed. While you are not personally responsible to make each person happy, only they can do that, you can create an environment in which they can succeed, be appreciated, and have a purpose. If you have the right people on your team, they will thrive in that atmosphere.

So, what does it mean to know your team? For starters, you can learn about their dreams and passions. Do they have a favorite hobby, have kids, or have an unusual family situation? Being aware of such things will help remove barriers that often arise between employees and leadership. It lets your people know that you are human, and that you care about more than just the job. Since the workplace is often too busy to have many personal conversations, we encourage you to plan social gatherings outside of the work environment. Host a dinner, a nature hike, go to a coffeehouse, or go bowling. Events such as these will allow you to see a different side of your people, and maybe even discover new talents that you could utilize at work.

Another positive side effect of hosting outside team activities is that it strengthens the personal relationships of the team as a whole. People who recreate outside of the work environment in a casual setting form stronger bonds. This can go a long way towards improving cohesiveness within the team, and increasing job satisfaction and enjoyment for each employee-which can only help all facets of your business.

There is another significant benefit to going below the surface of the work relationship. You will learn more of each person's personality, their communication style, learning style, likes, dislikes, and what motivates them. You can use this wealth of information in your coaching, and the effect is powerful. Remember the story we shared in lesson one about when we were co-managing a business, and had been tasked with growing the membership? We worked hard to reach our goals, but our work was not paying off. We turned things around using two powerful tools. We shifted the mindset of our team, and we coached each person based upon their communication and learning styles, and their personal motivators. We would have never been able to achieve our goals if we had not taken the time to get to know our team, and coaching them accordingly.

Here is a recap of some of the benefits of getting to know your team:

- You will become aware of each individual's learning style. This will help you to more effectively train, and assign job duties.

- You will learn how each person responds to coaching and feedback. Some people like the straightforward approach, while others need a softer touch.

- You will learn what motivates each individual. You may be surprised to discover that money is seldom a primary motivator. Often it is appreciation and recognition that really motivates a person to be a high performer. Knowing a person's primary motivators helps you customize their coaching and training.

- You will become aware of each individual's communication style. This will help you to manage more effectively, understand their behavior as well as identify future leadership potential.

- You will gain an understanding of each person's likes and dislikes. This will help you assign tasks, and identify areas where they could benefit from professional development.

You, as an owner or manager, will also benefit from getting to know your team because it will make you a more effective leader. Communication will be open and flow freely. There will be a foundation of trust, and your team will operate at a higher level knowing that you respect, honor, and value them. When you take the time to know what is important to your team members they will feel valued, and they will move mountains for you.

Real World Examples

Not Knowing Your Team: There are so many reasons why getting to know your team is important. When we first began leading a team of salespeople together, the owner wanted to increase sales, and tasked us with getting it done. We assessed the situation and discovered that the team had no real incentive to help them become more engaged. We met with the owner and suggested that we take into consideration the individual wants and needs of each person on the team. The owner, being a little impatient, decided to pass on that method and created a "one size fits all" incentive program. While there was nothing wrong with the program itself, it was not tailored to the people it was supposed to incentivize. Several weeks passed and the owner was pulling their hair out because they could not understand why the program was not working.

Knowing Your Team: While the owner was busy trying to make sense out of the fact that the new incentive program was not working, we were busy talking to each person on the team. We dug into what they really wanted, what made them happy and excited to come to work. In other words, we took the time to actually get to know our teammates. It was not easy, and it did not happen in a few days, but we designed new ways to incentivize the team, based upon their individual wants and needs. What do you think happened? Each person on the team began to recognize that we really cared about them, and that we cared about what made them happy. Do you know what happens when people know and believe that you care for them? They work very hard, and are happy to do so. In a matter of a few weeks sales began to skyrocket, and records were broken. Take note of this; the new program to incentivize the team was far less costly than the owners original plan. It is good to remember that money alone will never be a long-term incentive.

Lesson 4 Questions

- *Are you aware of the different personalities, and learning styles, of the people on your team?*

  Knowing each personality and learning style will allows better communication, and will make your training much more effective.

- *Do you know what motivates your team members to come into work every day? (Hint: It is seldom money alone.)*

  Take the time to discover specifically what it is that motivates each person on your team. For example: While everyone cares about money, some people place more value on being recognized for a job well done.

- *Do you know at least one personal thing about each person on your team?*

Effective leaders create personal connections.

Notes

Notes

"People rarely succeed unless they have fun in what they are doing."

~ Dale Carnegie
Writer, Lecturer,
Developer
of Self-Improvement
Courses

Lesson 5

Have Fun

Are your workdays filled with fun, or mired in stress and chaos? This lesson is all about the culture of your business. You can think of culture as being the mood, or attitude of your business, specifically of those who work within it. It is made up of the collective beliefs, attitudes, and values of each individual, including leadership personnel. Culture is a key component and it will impact the direction of the business. It will determine the quality of communication between all team members, as well as all business functions and decisions. Culture is so important that it will win over strategy every time.

Most every business will have an employee handbook, operations manual, or both. These resources are good for providing a framework and guidelines to employees working within a business. What those resources cannot do is prepare your team for every potential situation they will encounter, and that is where culture comes in. The culture within your business is what will guide your team through any situation not specifically outlined in the employee handbook, which is most situations. Your team will make hundreds of decisions on their own every week, and the culture of your business will determine the quality of those decisions. It will also determine if your team feels comfortable sharing their ideas, or even mistakes, with you. In other words, culture tells your team what to do, and how to behave, when the boss is not around.

Going to work should not be something your team dreads every day. In fact, it should be quite the opposite. Your team should enjoy the challenges, rewards, and the atmosphere that their job provides. The job itself may be difficult, but the atmosphere in which your team works should not provoke stress. In fact, the culture of your business should be intentionally designed to minimize stress. An atmosphere free of stress will result in happy employees, and happy employees mean lower turnover and higher performance. Happy employees also mean happy customers.

Understand that every business has a culture. It may be good, or it may be bad, but it exists. The only way to ensure your business has a good culture is to intentionally design it, and it begins with leadership. Leaders must embody and exemplify the values of the business. If a leader preaches to the team about punctuality, but is known for always being late, then the culture is being impacted negatively. If a leader emphasizes the importance of staying cool under pressure, and then demonstrates to the team that they can actually do that themselves, then the culture receives a positive impact. Leaders should be professional, but also compassionate, knowledgeable, flexible, and have a friendly disposition. Leaders should encourage transparency, open communication, and the freedom to innovate. Great leaders do more than delegate, they also participate. Great leaders are proficient at what they are asking others to do, and are not afraid to "get their hands dirty" by joining their team on the front lines when necessary.

Once the right leaders are in place, they can begin to assemble a team that fits the culture (see lesson 2 on hiring). Leaders also protect the culture by removing toxic individuals from the team quickly (see lesson 8 on firing). Do you know what happens when employees enjoy coming to work, look forward to seeing fellow team members, and know that they are valued and appreciated? They have fun, and a team that is having fun will grow your business exponentially.

A great culture is also a powerful recruiting tool. You will be amazed at how quickly word spreads about a business that has a great culture. Employees talk about it with their friends, and their friends tell other friends. When the time comes to fill a position, you will attract candidates who are better qualified and more skilled. Great cultures tend to attract great talent, and great talent builds a great business. A mediocre culture will attract mediocre talent, which will result in a mediocre business.

If you want to build a highly successful business that attracts good people, then get to work intentionally designing a culture that will make it happen.

Real World Examples

<u>No Fun:</u> This one is pretty simple. People who have no fun whatsoever at work, will not be happy people. Unhappy people will not take care of your customers, or their fellow coworkers. Many factors contribute to an unhappy atmosphere. Micromanaging, toxic people, lack of clarity and incentives are all things that were present when we first took leadership positions at the same business. The result was high turnover, low morale, lack of sales, and most everyone dreaded coming to work.

<u>Fun:</u> It took nearly a year for us to undo all of the damage that had been done, but when things turned around they turned around in a big way. We found that getting everyone together outside of work was a huge help. Once, we created a game out of who could make the best guacamole. We closed early one night, met offsite at someone's house and had our contest party. Everyone had a blast, and we even awarded

trophies to the top three winners. It was a small, simple idea, but one that paid huge dividends. There are so many things that you can do to ensure your business has a culture that is as fun as it is productive.

Lesson 5 Questions

- *Do you have fun at work? Does your team?*

  You likely spend more time with your coworkers than you do with your family. If you are not having fun, then there is a large chunk of your life where you are not happy.

- *Do you know what your team members consider to be fun?*

  Your idea of fun may differ from others on your team. Find out what they like.

- *Do you have outings with coworkers, which are not work related, in order to build team engagement?*

  Once you find out what kind of things your team considers to be fun, you can plan these outings.

- *What are some things you can do for fun that won't disrupt the productivity of the day?*

  When people can have fun, there will be less stress, higher productivity, lower turnover, and happier customers.

Notes

Notes

"This is a collaborative enterprise," she says. "You have to surround yourself with good people and help them to do what they do well, as opposed to micromanaging."

~ Robbie Myers
Editor-In-Chief of the
U.S. Edition the Fashion
Magazine
Elle

Micromanaging

The sure-fire way to smother the culture of your business, and the creativity of your team, is to be a micromanager. No one likes to be micromanaged. It is demotivating, frustrating, and discouraging. Do you know what has been said to be the number one contributor to happiness? Autonomy, which is pretty much the opposite of micromanagement.

Paying attention to details and holding team members accountable is an important part of being a manager, but these things can be done without hovering over every move your team makes. People want, and even need, to feel they are trusted to do their jobs. If they have their every decision brought into question, then they will stop making decisions and your business will grind to a halt. When you assign your team a project, step back and give them the freedom to make decisions, as well as mistakes. There may be a few bumps in the road at first, but in the end, offering your team autonomy will help build their leadership and problem-solving skills. This quote from General George. S. Patton sums things up nicely:

"Don't tell people how to do things, tell them what to do and let them surprise you with their results."

If you have a solid hiring process, and you have hired good people who fit well within your culture, then trust them to do their job. Simply assign them the task you want accomplished, set guidelines to let them know when you want it to be done, and then step back and let them do it. This can be easier said than done, but if you do it, you will be amazed at the level of creativity and drive your team will deploy in order to deliver the results. By not being a micromanager, you will free up yourself to focus on higher level activities that will keep the business moving forward.

There will be times when you have to step in and dictate certain steps that need to be taken, but if you find that you are doing that every day, and with every task, then you have either hired the wrong people or you are micromanaging.

If you find that it is you who is the micromanager in your business, don't beat yourself up or think that there is no hope. The attributes that lead to someone becoming a micromanager, attention to detail and being involved, are positive attributes. It is only when taken to the extreme that they become an issue.

Here are a few signs that you may be a micromanager:

- You focus on correcting minute details, rather than seeing the big picture.

- You have difficulty delegating tasks.

- You assign a task, and then involve yourself in every single step.

- You delegate a task, and then take it back because you found mistakes.

- You often begin sentences with, "I don't mean to micromanage, but…"

- You do not want others making a decision without consulting you first.

How do you stop being a micromanager? The first step is admitting it to yourself, and then to your team. Transparency will go a long way in repairing the damage caused by micromanaging. Let your team know you recognize it, and are committed to change. Assure them they have your upmost trust and confidence. Ask for their feedback, and accept it without feeling hurt. Remember, one of the most important traits of leadership is listening, so hear them out.

Moving forward, assign your team tasks, and then focus your own attention on the activities that will grow your business. Set up specific times with your team when they will give you updates on their progress. This will keep them accountable and give you the peace of mind that the task is being accomplished.

Real World Examples

Micromanaged: Once again we take an example from our experiences back when we were managing the same massage studio. When we assumed our roles as managers, the atmosphere of the business was one of fear with a dose of chaos. Why? Because everyone was being severely micromanaged. No one would make a decision, because they knew that no matter what they did, it would not be good enough. They feared the harsh criticism that came with every action they took, so they took no action. This, of course, resulted in chaos. The primary decision maker had made it clear that their decisions were the only right decisions. Every employee of that business knew that that they were not trusted to do things right.

Not Micromanaged: We knew there was only one way to turn things around, and that was to trust the people we had hired to do their job. Those that could not, or would not, we would have to replace. In the end, we did not have to replace anyone because we made it clear to them that we trusted them to work with autonomy, and to call on us only when needed. The result of all of this was that we created a bunch of leaders. Each person on our team was proactive and took initiative. They felt it was safe to share their ideas, and they had some fantastic ideas. By shifting away from an atmosphere dominated by micromanaging, everything else quickly improved.

Lesson 6 Questions

- *Are you constantly stressed, and no longer having fun when you are at work?*

  You could be a micromanager. Examine closely the reason why you are experiencing excessive stress.

- *Do you tell your team the exact way something needs to be done, and then get upset when the task was not completed to your exact expectations (even though the task was completed)?*

  Try this instead: Assign your team a task, but rather than describe in minute detail how you want it to be done, give them a date by which you would like it completed. Their creativity and zeal will amaze you.

- *How often do you ask your team the best way to achieve something?*

  You probably have a good understanding of every position in your business, but since you don't work each position daily, you may not understand it as well as one of your team members. Involve your team when setting goals or making policies.

Notes

Notes

"There are no mistakes or failures, only lessons."

~ Denis Waitley
Motivational Speaker, Writer, and Consultant.

Lesson 7

Mistakes Are Normal

When you are on a quest for excellence, it can be easy to forget that mistakes will happen. Every business owner or manager knows that mistakes, if they occur often, can be costly to the business, but they also know that mistakes are a normal byproduct of growth. In order to grow a business, it will be necessary to do things that have not been done before. When you and your team do things they have not done before, then mistakes will happen. The key is to learn from the mistakes and move on. Mistakes are not failures, they are stepping stones to success. Great leaders will allow room for their team to make mistakes, and then use those mistakes as a learning opportunity for the entire team.

As a leader in your business, you want to ensure your team knows that you will not get angry with them if they make a mistake. That said, you will also want to communicate that when a mistake is made, the person who made it must do the following:

- Own it.

- Learn from it, and share what they learned with the rest of the team.

- Fix it. Do everything in their power to resolve it as soon as possible.

- If they are unable to fix it, make their manager aware immediately so that it can be resolved.

- Work with the team to create a process that will prevent the same mistake being made again.

This mindset regarding mistakes in your business is an important part of your culture. If your team knows that they will not be ridiculed or humiliated for making a mistake, but are still held accountable, they will work hard to minimize mistakes. They will also work with you to co-create solutions to prevent making the same mistake in the future. This attitude toward mistakes encourages innovation and gives your team the courage to step out of their comfort zone.

Real World Examples

<u>Mistakes Ridiculed:</u> There was a person on our team who, in the beginning, would not hesitate to take action, make a decision, or try to

solve an issue on her own. Naturally, there were times when she would make a mistake. The primary leader of the business at that time would come down hard on any mistake that was made, and would make a case about it front of everyone. That harsh attitude toward mistakes took all of the wind from the sails of every person on the team. All initiative came to a halt because the only way to avoid making a mistake was to do nothing.

Mistakes Normal: When we took over the leadership of that team, we knew we had to make it clear that, unless the same mistake is continually made, making a mistake is completely normal. We would highlight our own mistakes and use them to coach the rest of the team. Doing this illustrated to the team that we too made mistakes, but used them as a learning tool. The result of this shift in attitude was that fewer mistakes were made, and the ones that were made were seldom repeated.

Lesson 7 Questions

- *Think about the last time you made a mistake. Did you hide the mistake or did you own it and learn from it?*

  Cast aside pride and demonstrate to your team how you handle mistakes.

- *If someone on your team makes a mistake, how do you deal with it?*

If a team member is repeatedly making the same mistake, then you may have to have a one-on-one meeting with them to determine why. If the mistake is due to inexperience, or lack of training, use the situation as a learning opportunity for everyone. This is especially effective, and transformational, when it is your own mistake that you use as a learning tool. Your team will respect you for it.

Notes

Notes

"Make sure everybody in your boat is rowing and not drilling holes when you're not looking. Know your circle."

~ Unknown

Lesson 8

The Firing Process

Firing someone is never easy, but it is sometimes necessary for the good of the business, and other team members. One of the most common mistakes caring leaders make is hanging on to an employee who is not contributing to the team. The effect this will have on the rest of the team, and the business overall, is never good. When we were co-managing a local massage franchise, we watched this play out right before our eyes. We had a relatively small team, about six people, and one of them had been resistant to any coaching we provided. This person had an extremely negative outlook on life in general, and we knew we needed to fire them. Finally, months later, we did fire that person, and do you know what happened? That same month our sales and closing ratio skyrocketed. We broke records, growth began to steadily climb every month, and we met goals months ahead of schedule. We had been coaching and deploying effective techniques for some time, but the influence of that one person held back the rest of our team and damaged our culture. When that influence was removed, the effect of our coaching took full effect, and the atmosphere was transformed.

The key is to ensure that you have given the individual every opportunity to succeed. Provide them the resources to do their job, as well as any coaching they need along the way. When they fall short of expectations, set up a one-on-one meeting with them. Discuss their performance and your expectations, and have them give you an action plan for their improvement. Be sure to document the meeting and the reason for it. Also, give the individual a deadline for improving their performance, with another meeting already scheduled for the review. Once that time has passed, and there has not been sufficient improvement, you may want to give them an official "write-up" along with the next date you will review their performance again. Let them know that if they have not met expectations by that time, you will have to let them go. Here are a few signs that it may be time to let someone go:

- Lack of enthusiasm and drive.

- A negative outlook and disposition.

- A poor fit into the business' culture.

- Complaints from customers.

- Frequently late to work, or no show.

- Resistant to coaching and change.

- Repeatedly not meeting expectations or goals.

- Constant complaining.

Whenever you delay removing a toxic individual from your team, you put at risk the rest of your team. Positivity is contagious, but so is negativity. The sooner you remove that influence from your business, the sooner you will see improvement. A good rule of thumb to use is this: If you find that in your management meetings you are continually talking about the same individual in a less than favorable light, then you have identified a person who may need to be let go.

Real World Examples

Not Firing: We had been managers a little over a year. We had experienced some growth in the business, but not nearly as much as we should have. About six months in, we knew there was one individual on the team that had to go. They were unresponsive to almost all of our coaching, had a negative attitude, and spent most of their time on the job complaining about most everything. The impact on our team was significant so we decided we would have to fire them. The owner resisted, because of the personal relationship they had developed, and overruled our decision. Months and months went by, and still our growth was stagnant. The morale of our team was getting lower by the day, and we were at our wits end.

Firing: Finally, we let the owner know that in order to grow the business as we had been tasked to do, we would have to fire the individual. Otherwise, there was no longer a need to pay us to manage the business. We got the green light and let the individual go. Four weeks later, a new record had been set for the number of memberships sold, and that was just the beginning. Morale improved, and other team members who had contemplated quitting, decided to stay.

Lesson 8 Questions

- *When you hold a manager's meeting, is there a particular team member that you find yourselves talking about talk about over and over, but not in a good way?*

If you are talking too much about a particular person (in a negative light) then it might be time for additional training, or for termination.

- *Do you have protocols in place for when someone is fired?*

  Each state has different labor laws regarding employment. You do not have to recite them all, but you do need to follow them all. Make sure you have yourself covered (proper documentation etc.), and have the proper protocols in place.

- *If you have to fire a team member who has been a negative influence, did you notice the ripple effect that action created?*

  Firing someone will have a ripple effect on your team, and if the person fired had been a negative influence, the ripple effect will be a positive one.

Notes

Notes

"Once you stop learning, you start dying."

~ Albert Einstein

Lesson 9

Train Continually

Any group of elite professionals, from Navy Seals to corporate executives, have one thing in common, and that is they never stop learning, growing and expanding their skills through continuous training. Nearly all of the skills needed to successfully operate a business are perishable, and need constant attention so that they remain sharp and consistent.

Most businesses understand the importance of training new employees, and typically invest a significant amount of time and money doing so. What many do not realize is that continuous training and development of their people is equally important. There are three primary reasons why:

- It will boost employee performance.

- It will increase employee satisfaction.

- It will pinpoint and strengthen areas of weakness.

Chances are that you have invested a lot of time and resources into finding, and hiring, a good team. Because humans have a need to feel that they are progressing, growing your team through ongoing training will help reduce turnover, and the frustration of having to start the hiring process all over again. One reason why many business owners, or their managers, are resistant to creating an ongoing training program is the perception that it will be time consuming, but what must be pointed out is that no other investment you can make will do more to increase the productivity of your team.

The best place to start training your team is on the skills they need to perform their daily tasks. The more they train on these things, the more efficient they become, and soon those skills become second nature. Once your team has mastered the basics of their jobs, help them level up to more responsibilities and rewards by adding new skills to their arsenal.

When it comes training new hires, there is no reason why you have to be the only one doing it. In fact, if you tap into the talented people you already have working for you, you will not only get the new person up to speed quicker, but you will also instill in them the culture of the business. Peer coaching is a powerful tool and one you should utilize often. The new hire is not the only one who will benefit from this type of coaching. The experienced team member who is doing the coaching will further enhance their skills, as well as maintain a higher level of engagement. Engaged employees will perform better, and stay longer.

Real World Examples

No Regular Training: Early in our time as co-managers, we were not training our people on a regular basis. We would role play occasionally, or address certain topics at our quarterly staff meetings, but that was about it. We struggled to increase sales, and perfect other skills, but it took us a while to fully understand the need for ongoing training. So, closing ratios and growth were far below our expectations.

Ongoing Training: Eventually, we came to realize that in every profession there are those individuals who are able to consistently perform at a high level. Those people, we noted, never ceased to train. In fact, training was a lifestyle for them. We made the decision that we would bring that concept into the business we were responsible for managing. No longer was training an intermittent activity, but something we engaged in every day. We created a daily atmosphere of learning and sharing. We encouraged all of our team members to practice their skills every day, and to share with others what they had learned.

Doing this doubled the number of people coaching, as the team was now also learning from each other, and not just management. The result was a team of highly professional and skilled people who performed at a high level, and did so consistently.

Lesson 9 Questions

- *Do you have an ongoing training system in place?*

  Every elite performer, whether they are a soldier, athlete, or salesperson, continues training on a regular basis. Most learned skills are perishable, and need to be trained often in order to remain sharp.

- *Do you have an evaluation process in place?*

  Tracking each person's performance will allow you to see areas for improvement, and will give you advance warning of issues affecting performance.

- *Who is responsible for training?*

Owners and managers do not have to be the only people doing the training. If you have highly experienced people on your team, you can delegate some of the training to them. We call this Peer Coaching, and it is very effective.

Notes

Notes

"If we don't make the time to celebrate the moments in our lives, it will feel less meaningful and special...."

~ Stephanie Zamora
Author

Lesson 10

Celebrate the Victories

It is easy to quickly move on to the next task after your team accomplishes a goal, but when your team scores a win, it is important that you recognize it. Be sure to celebrate small wins as often as you do bigger ones. Big wins are typically few and far between, so celebrating the smaller wins will keep your team positive and engaged. As a leader you must be able to recognize how important recognition is to you and your team. Recognition, both public and private, will motivate and energize your team because it shows them you appreciate the progress they have made. If you have taken the time to get to know your team (lesson 4) as a leader you will be able to customize the recognition to your team members.

Here are just a few of the benefits of celebrating victories with your team:

- **Inspires your team to continue delivering high performance.** When your team feels their hard work has been appreciated, they will likely work even harder on the next goal.

- **It focuses your team's attention on the positive.** Negative things happen, and it is all too easy for your team to focus on those things. By celebrating a victory, no matter how small, it will keep your team focused on the positive things that are happening.

- **It builds momentum.** When you celebrate a win, your team is reminded that they have what it takes to accomplish a goal. So, when the next goal is presented to them, they go after it with the knowledge that they can accomplish it because they have done it before.

- **It unifies the team.** When a group of people accomplish something together, that group of people become tighter, closer, and will think as a team, not just a group of individuals.

- **It allows you an opportunity to recognize specific employees and reward them.** Doing this reinforces to the rest of the team the kind of behaviors and attitudes that are valued within your culture.

These celebrations can be on site, or off, but the importance of them cannot be overstated. Be sure to allow your team to share during these times. Encourage each person to share their thoughts on why the team was successful, and what they believe is necessary to continue winning. You will learn a lot about your team this way, and your team will learn a lot about each other.

Real World Examples

No Celebrating: Once you have built a hard-working team of people, you must allow them to enjoy their victories. We learned the importance of this the hard way. We were hard at work building a high-performing sales team that were also rock stars of customer service. We began reaching goal after goal, but after a while it seemed our team was losing some steam. We investigated why this was happening, and what we discovered was an eye-opener. The team did not feel like their hard work was being recognized.

Celebrating: We knew they were right, and we knew we were going to do something about it. We appointed two of our team members as activities coordinators. Their job was to come up with ways for us to celebrate and have fun. They embraced their roles with enthusiasm, and the entire group of employees were eager to participate. These times of celebration were talked about long after they were over, and left everyone looking forward to the next one. The result was improved morale and goals were once again being reached. People need to feel appreciated and they need the time to pause and celebrate a win.

Lesson 10 Questions

- *Do you remember the last time you congratulated a team member on a victory?*

  Acknowledging victories, even small ones, will show your team that you are grateful for their hard work. It will also increase their confidence, as well as help build a culture of appreciation.

- *Do you have big celebrations for big goals?*

  Daily and weekly acknowledgment of small victories is important, but be sure to plan something special for when your team hits those big goals. Make sure your team is aware of what the reward will be, and they will work together to achieve it.

- *Do you encourage your team to congratulate each other for a job well done?*

The best way to do this is to lead by example. Peer to peer recognition is one of the most understated forms of reward. Do you have a system in place that will allow your team to congratulate and recognize each other?

Notes

Notes

The Take-Away

Implement

You just read ten important lessons that will transform you, your team, and your business. If they are embraced and applied, these lessons will increase the success of your business, as well as the success of every member of your team. Now is your opportunity to build momentum through practical application. Pick a lesson, and then find ways to apply it to your situation. Then, pick another and then another. Soon, you will see a significant change come over your business. Will you make mistakes? Of course. Will it always be easy? No. Will it be worth it? Absolutely.

Notes

Notes

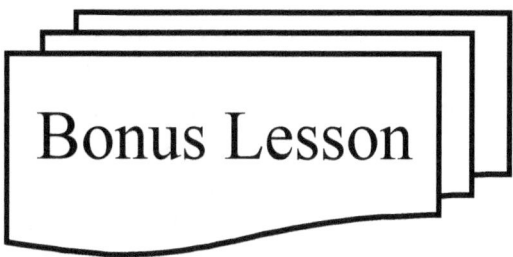

Bonus Lesson

Communication

Good communication within your business is essential if you intend to build a team that will make the business successful. Without good communication it will be nearly impossible for you team to work toward the same goals. It is the leadership of a business that must create a culture of effective communication, because if the leaders are poor communicators, then you can expect everyone else to follow their example. Self-awareness is the key, so before you hire, fire, train, or discipline anyone you should take an honest look at the effectiveness of your style of communication. If you discover that the way you are communicating to your staff is ineffective, then it is imperative that you develop an action plan to remedy that as soon as possible, otherwise the business will not achieve a significant level of success.

Each person working in your business will have their favorite way to communicate. Some of them will prefer texting, others email, and still others a phone call. Because of this, it is important to set some ground rules for the way your team communicates with each other, and with you, otherwise you will have chaos. We suggest setting this expectation when you first hire someone, that way it is clear from the beginning. In Lesson 4 we discussed the importance of getting to know your team. Creating an effective plan for communicating is one more reason why that lesson is so important. If you really get to know each person on your team, you will discover the most effective way to communicate with each one. You will have some who use text as a primary form of communicating. Others will almost always use email. Whatever method they use, it is up to you to adapt and map out a plan with each person, and then stick to it. As a leader, you must meet your people where they are, not where you wish they were. Do this, and you will reap the rewards of a business that knows how to communicate.

Here are some important things to remember when it comes to communication:

- Once you have nailed down a plan for communicating with your team, the next thing you must remember is to always follow through. If you do not follow through the employee will lose trust in you.

- Respond in a timely manner. If you do not have time to respond properly, then communicate that to your people. Let them know that you are tied up, but will respond as soon as you are able. Also, give them a time frame within which they can expect your answer.

- Follow through on statements that you make. If you tell your team you will do something, make sure you do it, or explain to them why you were unable to do so. There is little more than can cause your people to lose their trust in you than making promises you do not keep. It is easier to gain and keep someone's trust than to rebuild it.

- If you do not know something, it is okay to admit you do not know. Transparency will cause your team to trust and respect you even more. The key is, once you have admitted to not knowing, is to let them know you will find the answer. Do this, and your staff will have confidence in your leadership skills.

What happens when you have poor communication? You staff will not respect or trust your ability to effectively and successfully run the business. A leader that communicates well, and creates an atmosphere of clear communication, will have a team that will perform well at every level. Processes will be easier, goals will be met, and the quality of service provided to your customers will be unsurpassed.

The Hard Stuff

When you are in a leadership role within a business, you must create a culture that allows for difficult topics to be discussed without animosity. Whether the conversation is between managers and employees, owners and managers, or any combination thereof, the ability to have constructive conversations around challenging topics is imperative. If everyone is afraid to open up a discussion about something because they think the other person will get mad, everything will suffer. The business will suffer, and so will the morale of everyone who works there. Of course, you will want to approach such conversations with tact, but walking around on eggshells serves no one.

Bonus Lesson Questions

- *Do you know how to effectively communicate with your team?*

  Styles of communication differ with each team member. Some will prefer to communicate via phone and email, while others may prefer to text everything. Remember, there is no wrong way to communicate, but not communicating is wrong. Find out each person's preferred method, and if you decide to have one primary way to communicate with your team, make them aware of it.

- *Does your team know how to communicate effectively with you?*

  In the same way that you need to know how to best communicate with your team, they need to know how to best communicate with you.

- *Do you have protocols in place in case of an emergency?*

  Whether it be a weather emergency, or something more serious, be sure to have protocols in place that will allow every person on your team to know what is going on.

Notes

Notes

One More Thing

Feelings Win Every Time

Though it has been alluded to several times throughout this book, the culture of your business is of utmost importance. Business culture is more than merely beliefs, behaviors, and processes. It is the way you and your people *feel* while you are at work. Most people spend a significant portion of their lives at work, so it is important that the environment in which they work be a good one.

It is the attitude of each and every person in the business that will shape the working environment. A positive workplace environment is a crucial factor in employee satisfaction, and will have a direct effect on your bottom line. If you and your people are happy, you will make your customers happy. If your customers are happy they will continue to do business with you.

The atmosphere of any business begins with the leadership of that business. If you are reading this book then you are probably in a leadership role, so it is important for you to know that your disposition will greatly influence every person on your team. Negativity is contagious, but so is positivity. Here are a few signs that you may need to improve your business culture:

- High turnover- If you find that you are continually losing people, especially your top performers, then it may be due to a poor work environment.

- Lack of interaction- If you notice that the people in your business are not socially interacting with each other, and choose silence over communication, then they may not be happy at work.

- Reluctance to make decisions- If you see that your people choose to not act, or make decisions, then it is likely they are not engaged. People who are not engaged are not enjoying what they do.

- Conflict- While not everyone will agree all of the time, it is the way in which they disagree that will demonstrate whether the culture of a business is good or bad. Happy and engaged people will focus on finding the best solution. Unhappy and disengaged people will be more concerned about being right, or winning an argument.

How people feel will win over strategy, training and "best practices" every time. Remember, a business is made up of people, and those same people will determine what type of culture the business will have. Leaders must set the example, and then hire other people who best fit the desired culture. It should be noted that culture is not something you simply create once and then you are done. A great culture must be intentionally created, and then intentionally protected.

Notes

Notes

Notes

Notes

Learn more about how you can build your team
and grow your business at

WinningMindsetConsulting.com

Contact Keith or Mandy via email at
info@winningmindsetconsulting.com

Who We Are

We are a coaching and consulting company with a passion for helping businesses grow. We have spent years on the front lines developing real solutions for:

- Increasing the sales effectiveness of your front desk staff.

- Growing & retaining members and clients.

- Streamlined & effective processes for the day to day operations of your business.

- Building & sustaining a culture that supports the growth of your business.

This book was written as a basic guide to the more in-depth consulting and training we provide for our clients. No matter what growth challenges you are facing, we have years of expertise in overcoming them. Whether it is lack of sales, a negative work environment, difficulty hiring the right people, or lack of organization around key tasks, we deliver results. Our work is based on experience, not theory.

We Build Teams That Win!

Acknowledgments

We have learned from and been helped by several people thoughout the process of creating this book. We wish to acknowledge these individuals here:

Eric Brown for freely sharing with us from his vast storehouse of wisdom. We have learned so much from him.

Millie Case-Herndon for demonstrating the meaning and power of loyalty, dependability and hard work.

Amanda Chism for her dedication to self-improvement, and for aptly demonstrating what it means to care for others.

Jenny Ellis for all of her insights and hard work editing this book. Without her it would not have been possible.

Tammy Kling for selflessly making herself available to coach, inspire, and encourage us to follow our dream.

Jenny Larsen for creating the logo for Winning Mindset Consulting, and for her tremendous amount of skill and creativity.

Allison McGarry for her ability to make nearly every situation fun, and for exemplifying the true joy of living.

"It's not the end of the book, it's just the beginning of a new chapter."

~ Unknown